Effective Heads
of
Department

Phil Jones
and
Nick Sparks

Published by Network Educational Press Ltd
PO Box 635
Stafford
ST16 1BF

First Published 1996
© Phil Jones & Nick Sparks 1996

ISBN 1 85539 036 1

Phil Jones & Nick Sparks assert the moral right to be identified
as the authors of this work

Series Editor - Professor Tim Brighouse
Edited by Sara Peach
Design & layout by
Neil Hawkins of Devine Design
Illustrations by Joe Rice

Printed in Great Britain by
Redwood Books, Trowbridge, Wilts.

Foreword

A teacher's task is much more ambitious than it used to be and demands a focus on the subtleties of teaching and learning and on the emerging knowledge of school improvement.

This is what this series is about.

Teaching can be a very lonely activity. The time honoured practice of a single teacher working alone in the classroom is still the norm; yet to operate alone is, in the end to become isolated and impoverished. This series addresses two issues - the need to focus on practical and useful ideas connected with teaching and learning and the wish thereby to provide some sort of an antidote to the loneliness of the long distance teacher who is daily berated by an anxious society.

Teachers flourish best when, in key stage teams or departments (or more rarely whole schools), their talk is predominantly about teaching and learning and where, unconnected with appraisal, they are privileged to observe each other teach; to plan and review their work together; and to practise the habit of learning from each other new teaching techniques. But how does this state of affairs arise? Is it to do with the way staffrooms are physically organised so that the walls bear testimony to interesting articles and in the corner there is a dedicated computer tuned to 'conferences' about SEN, school improvement, the teaching of English etc, and whether, in consequence, the teacher leaning over the shoulder of the enthusiastic IT colleagues sees the promise of interesting practice elsewhere? Has the primary school cracked it when it organises successive staff meetings in different classrooms and invites the 'host' teacher to start the meeting with a 15 minute exposition of their classroom organisation and management? Or is it the same staff sharing, on a rota basis, a slot on successive staff meeting agenda when each in turn reviews a new book they have used with their class? And what of the whole school which now uses 'active' and 'passive' concerts of carefully chosen music as part of their accelerated learning techniques?

It is of course well understood that excellent teachers feel threatened when first they are observed. Hence the epidemic of trauma associated with OFSTED. The constant observation of the teacher in training seems like that of the learner driver. Once you have passed your test and can drive unaccompanied, you do. You often make lots of mistakes and sometimes get into bad habits. Woe betide, however, the back seat driver who tells you so. In the same way the new teacher quickly loses the habit of observing others and being observed. So how do we get a confident, mutual observation debate going? One school I know found a simple and therefore brilliant solution. The Head of the History Department asked that a young colleague plan lessons for her - the Head of Department - to teach. This lesson she then taught and was observed by the young colleague. The subsequent discussion, in which the young teacher asked,

"Why did you divert the question and answer session I had planned?"
and was answered by,
"Because I could see that I needed to arrest the attention of the group by the window with some hands on role play, etc."

lasted an hour and led to a once-a-term repeat discussion which, in the end, was adopted by the whole school. The whole school subsequently changed the pattern of its meetings to consolidate extended debate about teaching and learning. The two teachers claimed that because one planned and the other taught both were implicated but neither alone was responsible or felt 'got at'.

So there are practices which are both practical and more likely to make teaching a rewarding and successful activity. They can, as it were, increase the likelihood of a teacher surprising the pupils into understanding or doing something they did not think they could do rather than simply entertaining them or worse still occupying them. There are ways of helping teachers judge the best method of getting pupil expectation just ahead of self-esteem.

This series focuses on straightforward interventions which individual schools and teachers use to make life more rewarding for themselves and those they teach. Teachers deserve nothing less for they are the architects of tomorrow's society and society's ambition for what they achieve increases as each year passes.

Professor Tim Brighouse.

Contents

INTRODUCTION

The purpose of this book is quite simply to support Heads of Department in getting the best from their team and in so doing enhance the performance of the pupils they teach. The contents may also be of interest to Senior Managers who are endeavouring to support the development of key members of their school's middle management.

As schools become ever more accountable, so an increasing challenge is placed on those in key roles in schools to perform at even higher levels. The Head of Department occupies one of those roles. The publication of test scores, examination results and OFSTED inspection reports has led to growing expectations of Heads of Department to deliver high quality results.

These demands, coupled with a rapidly changing curriculum, have resulted in the need for Heads of Departments to be proficient in a much wider range of management skills than ever used to be the case. The following lists of questions taken from interviews for Head of Department posts in 1976 and in 1996 illustrate the point well.

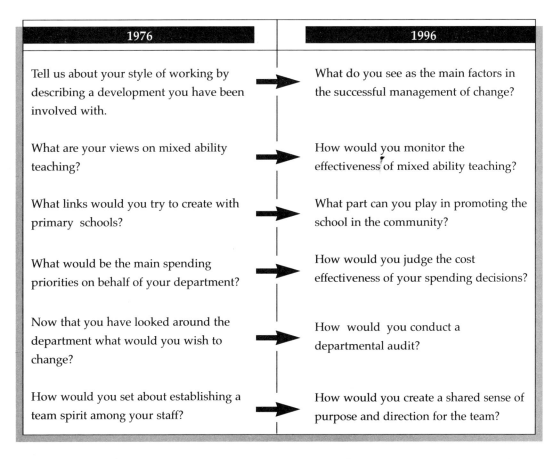

1976	1996
Tell us about your style of working by describing a development you have been involved with.	What do you see as the main factors in the successful management of change?
What are your views on mixed ability teaching?	How would you monitor the effectiveness of mixed ability teaching?
What links would you try to create with primary schools?	What part can you play in promoting the school in the community?
What would be the main spending priorities on behalf of your department?	How would you judge the cost effectiveness of your spending decisions?
Now that you have looked around the department what would you wish to change?	How would you conduct a departmental audit?
How would you set about establishing a team spirit among your staff?	How would you create a shared sense of purpose and direction for the team?

The content of the 1996 questions clearly demonstrates the need for today's Head of Department to be an effective manager regardless of which department he or she manages. The concepts of 'management of change', 'monitoring', 'evaluating', 'effectiveness' and 'audit' are firmly established as key features of the role. This book aims to support Heads of Department in the development of these and other skills, so that they may become more effective as managers, to the benefit of their colleagues and pupils.

Section One

Effective Departmental Planning

> **In Section One you will learn that:**
>
> ☞ **Planning is vital to a successful department**
>
> ☞ **Both the curriculum and the development of the department need to be planned**
>
> ☞ **Planning needs to take place in the short, medium and long terms**
>
> ☞ **Departments have to plan learning experiences and learning intentions**

Effective planning is a vital component of the successful department. The right planning processes form a key element in the drive to guarantee quality. Equally importantly, they provide an effective way of managing change. At their best, the ways in which a department plans can provide the security that staff need, in order to know that they are delivering what is expected and that the department is moving in the right direction. When planning processes are faulty or insecure, consistency is hard to maintain and much staff time and energy can be wasted on low and disparate priority issues. This causes frustration and that demoralising 'not coping' feeling.

There are two key dimensions to department planning:
- Curriculum planning
- Development planning

Curriculum Planning

Curriculum planning is the process by which the department ensures that all pupils receive the curriculum teaching to which they are entitled. Planning will be based initially on the need to deliver several key elements which could include:

- National Curriculum programmes of study
- Examination syllabus requirements
- Cross-curricular elements agreed within the school
- Any other specific areas of content or process deemed by the department to be important
- Whole school and departmental OFSTED targets
- Provision of differentiated learning targets

In order to be effective, the Head of Department needs to ensure that each of these has been considered in terms of three stages of planning:

- Long term
- Medium term
- Short term

		Year 7	Year 8	Year 9
Autumn Term	half term	Medieval Realms	The Making of the UK Part II	Britain 1750-1900
	half term			
Spring Term	half term		The French Revolution	Local Study Cromford
	half term			
Summer Term	half term	The Making of the UK Part I	Black Peoples of America	20th Century World
	half term			

Each of theses stages is important in its own right and the Head of Department needs to work with his or her department staff to establish a process which incorporates all three. As with any aspect of the work of a department, the more that the staff work together to form an agreed consensus about the purpose and value of whatever processes the department adopts, the more effective they are likely to be.

Long term planning

This constitutes the broad outline of what will be taught each term, year and Key Stage. At its simplest it will be a series of titles of units of work or topics to be covered. More helpfully these will be fixed into a time frame giving a clear indication of when each unit will be taught and for what duration of time. An example of a long term plan for History at Key Stage 3 might look like the plan on the previous page.

A similar plan, covering Key Stages Three and Four (and the Sixth Form where appropriate) provides security in a range of ways for the Head of Department and their departmental staff:

> ✓ **all key areas of the curriculum are being covered**
> ✓ **there is a broadly appropriate time allocation for each unit of work**
> ✓ **teachers know what is to be covered and by when**
> ✓ **appropriate resources can be made available at the right time**
> ✓ **field trips and visitors can be arranged well in advance**

Medium term planning

The medium term plan takes each unit of work in turn and describes it in terms of its key features. It should not be so detailed becomes a chore to look through, and make sense of, or that it is seen by teachers as a straitjacket.

All teachers need to be given some flexibility in what they teach and the way in which they teach it. One of the great problems with the National Curriculum in its early days was that teachers saw it as taking away an important element of their professionalism. They were being told everything that they had to do. A departmental medium term plan should not fall in to this trap.

On the other hand, a key purpose of good planning is that it forms the basis of a guarantee for pupils of what they are entitled to receive, no matter which member of the department's staff is teaching them. This balance between over-prescription and entitlement is an important one to strike. Every unit of work cannot be tackled in this way, all at once, but there should be a rolling programme, so that over time, each unit is reviewed and a medium term plan agreed.

In constructing the plan for each unit, 7 key questions should be answered:

✓ 1   What has to be covered as a statutory requirement?
✓ 2   What are the key questions pupils should investigate?
✓ 3   What should pupils know, understand and be able to do by the end of the unit?
✓ 4   Is there appropriate provision for differentiation?
✓ 5   Are there particular activities which all pupils should experience?
✓ 6   Are there particular resources that all pupils should have experience of using?
✓ 7   What key assessments should be undertaken?

These questions enable the Head of Department to ensure the provision of a quality experience for all pupils without being too restrictive for the teacher. The most effective and economical way of expressing the answers to these questions in the form of a grid or matrix. We suggest that in order to make this manageable, the medium term plan for each unit should comprise two grids, each one on a side of A4 (as illustrated on pages 14 & 16) and entitled:

- Learning Experiences
- Learning Intentions

Learning Experiences

The matrix on page 14 should indicate those aspects of the unit of work which the department has decided are 'entitlement experiences' for all pupils. Of course pupils will do other things but this matrix records the core of the unit; those things the children will experience no matter which teacher they have. It is, as far as the Head of Department is concerned, the bottom line and will act as an important benchmark when he or she monitors the quality of pupils' experiences within the department. The headings for the matrix have been chosen for the following reasons:

1. Key Questions

Because most topics or units, no matter what the subject, can be sub-divided into a series of questions. If these are used as the focus for pupils' work, then they are more likely to be involved in enquiry-based learning, research and problem solving. These questions need to be carefully linked to National Curriculum programmes of study, and examination syllabuses and the locally agreed syllabus.

2. Key Activities

Because the department should be committed to including a range of teaching and learning styles as part of all pupils' entitlement. This part of the matrix should highlight those key activities which the department feels will deliver the range that pupils are entitled to within this particular unit. We all know that there can be a tendency for some teachers to avoid some kinds of activities-for a variety of reasons. Sadly this can mean that some groups of pupils receive a significantly different and less rich experience within the same subject area. The effective Head of Department will want to reduce the chances of this occurin to a minimum and the key activities part of the matrix provides support for this.

3. Key Resources

Because there will often be a range of resources available beyond whatever standard text or worksheets the department uses. This part of the matrix reminds staff of what is available in order to enhance the learning experience of pupils and signals the expectation that they will be used.

4. Focus Elements

Because in each unit of work there will be particular elements of the National Curriculum or syllabus that are appropriate to address. These will often be specific Attainment Targets or objectives within a syllabus.

5. Assessment Opportunities

Because it is helpful to signal at what point key assessments should be made to ensure that opportunities are created to make judgements about pupil progress. The department should, of course, be looking to incorporate a variety of assessment methods and this provides an opportunity to ensure that such a variety is planned in. Additionally, if these assessments are common and undertaken at agreed points in time it will assist the department in generating data that can help it analyse its effectiveness (see Section 2 on assessment).

The Learning Experiences Grid

Topic / Unit:

Key Questions	Key Activities	Key Resources	Focus Elements	Assessment Opportunities

Another advantage for the Head of Department who plans in this way is that the matrices provide a relatively simple method of providing answers to the following questions:

✎ What is the range of teaching and learning experiences which children are exposed to?

✎ What is the range of resources which they experience?

✎ What is the variety of assessment methods we use within the department?

These are instructive questions which get to the heart of the department's work. The answers can provide information on where further development is needed.

Learning Intentions

When we teach a unit of work it is essential that we have a clear view of what we want the pupils to learn. This may seem obvious, but given large amounts of curriculum content to cover it is all to easy to resort to ploughing through a mass of content simply to try to get coverage. Sadly we know that this race through content is often satisfying to neither pupil nor teacher. Completing the Learning Intentions Grid gives us an opportunity to be more focused about what we intend pupils with different abilities to achieve as a result of having undertaken a specific unit of work.

The Learning Intentions Grid asks the following questions:

 What do we intend pupils to know, understand and be able to do by the end of this unit?

In this context, knowledge is perhaps best expressed as pieces of information for factual recall; understanding relates to the concepts about which pupils should be able to articulate reasons and explanations and the 'be able to do' column is obviously for those key skills which pupils need to develop.

The layout of the grid has been designed to aid differentiation in that it asks the department to consider the following three questions:

✎ What must all pupils who undertake this unit, even the least able, be expected to know, understand and be able to do?

✎ What should most pupils be able to achieve? These items might not be achievable by the least able.

✎ What in addition might the most able be expected to achieve?

We suggest that a department wishing to develop a matrix of this kind should start by taking one unit of work and simply addressing the 'most' part of the grid. This will

The Learning Intentions Grid

Topic / Unit:

	Know	Understand	Be able to
All Pupils Must			
Most Pupils Should			
Some Pupils Could			

give a feel for the method. Then it is really a question of considering what to expect of the extremes of the ability range. How do we ensure that the least able are helped to understand the key material? How often do we give the most able opportunities to use the key material as the basis for further research and development?

This grid should be over-detailed. It should not contain only the key elements of knowledge, understanding and skills. Some boxes may well only contain one or two elements, although as they progress through the unit, pupils will no doubt achieve more than the grid contains.

The power of such a grid is twofold. In the first place it enables the teacher to ensure that classroom activities are focused on the delivery of the learning intentions - if this is what pupils must get out of the unit then what activities will best deliver it? Secondly, the grid should guide a major part of the department's assessment.

Taken together, the Learning Experiences Grid and the Learning Intentions Grid provide a secure basis for any department's medium term planning, by providing a manageable vehicle for planning and evaluation.

Short Term Planning

This is the kind of planning that needs to be done on a week-by-week or day-by-day basis. It is, to a large degree, the fine tuning undertaken by individual teachers in response to the way in which classes and individual pupils progress with each unit of work. The Head of Department will want to have discussed with their department how effective short term planning can make a real difference to pupils' achievements. When done well, this type of planning ensures that teachers keep track of the successes and failures of those they are teaching and adapt their approaches and materials appropriately. In short it can make a big contribution to good differentiation.

So, what should teachers be doing in terms of short term planning? There are two questions to which the Head of Department needs to provide answers:

✎ **What needs to be recorded?**
For each group being taught the following items will be helpful:
- Where is the group up to?
- What do we need to move on to next?
- What has proved difficult for them?
- Are any important pieces of intended learning insecure and so need further work?
- Are individual pupils having difficulty?
- What needs to be done?
- Are some individuals doing particularly well and so need moving on more quickly?
- Do I need to have any specific resources available for next session?

✎ **Where and when should it be recorded?**
Clearly the responses to the above questions will best be jotted down by the teacher in his or her own notebook. They will often be written during a lesson as something becomes apparent or towards the end of the session. Occasionally a teacher might reflect at a later time on some aspect of the

lesson and add something . But it is not intended that this kind of planning becomes an onerous task undertaken at length out of school hours. They are by and large on-going jottings and reminders which will enhance the way in which a teacher approaches subsequent lessons with any group.

Because good short term planning can be powerful in enhancing the quality of what happens in the classroom, the Head of Department cannot leave this to chance. In order to ensure that it is happening the Head of Department might:

- Issue all department staff with short term planning note books
- Agree with the department how they are to be used and what they should contain
- Occasionally, as part of the programme of monitoring quality in the department, have a look at the way in which they are being used
- Share any examples of good practice
- Address any real concerns on the part of staff about their use.

Development Planning

Most schools are now familiar with the need for an annual cycle of planning and review. Indeed many schools now have sophisticated mechanisms for planning over the long, medium and short term with respect to whole school issues. It is important that the Head of Department is also equipped to plan effectively for the development of the department over time.

This is not planning for its own sake or just filling in bits of paper to satisfy either the Head Teacher or Ofsted. The effective Head of Department uses department development planning for a variety of important and highly practical reasons. The major benefits are explored below.

It allows development work to be paced over a reasonable period of time

The quantity of change which departments have had to cope with over recent years needs no elaboration here. Equally we know that things are unlikely to stand still in the foreseeable future. With all this change it would not be difficult for a Head of Department to feel submerged by all that needs to be done and to not know quite which way to turn. One major purpose of the development plan is to enable the Head of Department to feel that things are under control and that sanity can be maintained!

We suggest that a department tries to project its work over a period of three years. This means that there is a need for some serious prioritisation. Helpful questions are:

- What needs to be in place either during or by the end of this year?
- What is desirable but can be delayed until either next year or the year after?
- What do we not really need to be concerned with?

The answers to these questions could be determined by a variety of factors such as:

- Whole school requirements
- National Curriculum or syllabus demands
- Department staff needs
- The department's own development agenda
- OFSTED action plans

Nevertheless there is often a need to be ruthless in the prioritisation process. We cannot be expected to do everything and certainly not all at once. You should be able to construct a timeline spreading over 3 years which denotes priority developments (see the example on page 20). Your department staff will welcome a measured approach to development.

It promotes collaboration amongst department staff
The development plan should not be the product solely of the work of the Head of Department. Of course, leadership will be needed and perhaps a rough first draft will get the debate going. But the best plans and those that have the greatest chance of successful implementation will be generated through discussion by the department as a whole. The discussion will require clear steerage and in this the following questions will be helpful:

- What are the things we must do?
- What are the things we would like to do?
- When do they need to be done by?
- What resources will be required to enable them to be done?
- Which of us could oversee each development and who could make contributions to it?
- What benefits will each development bring to the work of the department?

If this process is followed it should ensure that staff feel some ownership of the plan and there will be a clarity about the purpose of the different elements within it.

It promotes the best use of staff talents and professional development
A Head of Department cannot do everything and most teachers are willing to take a share of development work as long as the load is reasonable, given sufficient time and is well supported by the Head of Department. A well constructed plan allows staff to opt in to those pieces of work where they have a strength or where they feel they wish to develop themselves. For some, though not all, this will be the kind of opportunity they want, to be responsible for the development of some important aspect of the department's work.

Department Development Plan

Development Target	Timeline	Financial Implications	Success Criteria	Staff Responsible

It encourages the best use of scarce financial resources

The management of finance is dealt with in detail elsewhere in this book but the linking of relevant aspects of the plan to their financial implications is important. Few developments have no cost and most departments have to make the most of a relatively small financial allocation. This is all the more reason to make sure that whatever finance is available is securely linked to department priorities.

Additionally, the costing of longer term developments can alert Senior Managers to future financial needs. Costs might be related to:

- The purchase of resources
- Staff supply cover for INSET
- Course fees

It encourages the department to think clearly about the potential benefits for pupils of any development

The department needs to be reasonably clear about what it expects to get out of any development. This clarity is most usefully expressed in terms of the impact the level should have on pupil outcome. Essentially, if it is not going to make a difference to quality and achievement, then it's probably not worth doing. The sharper the department can be at describing 'success criteria' the more effective the development is likely to be. The key attribute of good success criteria is that they lend themselves to being measured in some way so that there is clear evidence of them having been achieved. The Head of Department will, of course, ensure that the plan is realistic, in the sense that the targets set are achievable, given the resources, and are available. There is nothing so dispiriting as having set a whole string of targets which a team fails to achieve.

The best plans become working documents for the department. These are regularly referred to in department meetings or in discussions with Senior Managers.

One department we saw recently had used the photocopier to enlarge the plan and put it on the wall of their workroom. As parts of it were achieved they were highlighted in a colour and progress with the plan was reviewed each half term. We were told that they saw the plan as their **'Record of Achievement'**.

An example of a suggested layout for a department development plan is illustrated below but remember, it's not the piece of paper or the particular layout that you adopt that matters. It is rather the processes that the department adopts that will enhance the work of the department.

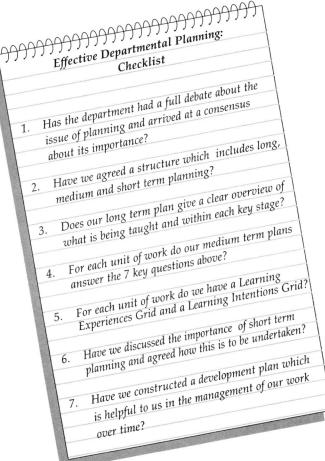

Effective Departmental Planning: Checklist

1. Has the department had a full debate about the issue of planning and arrived at a consensus about its importance?

2. Have we agreed a structure which includes long, medium and short term planning?

3. Does our long term plan give a clear overview of what is being taught and within each key stage?

4. For each unit of work do our medium term plans answer the 7 key questions above?

5. For each unit of work do we have a Learning Experiences Grid and a Learning Intentions Grid?

6. Have we discussed the importance of short term planning and agreed how this is to be undertaken?

7. Have we constructed a development plan which is helpful to us in the management of our work over time?

Making Assessment Valuable

> **In Section Two you will learn that:**
>
> ☞ **Assessment needs to focus on:**
>
> > - knowing how well pupils are doing
> >
> > - knowing how well the department is doing
>
> ☞ **Examination data can tell us about the performance of**
>
> > - individual pupils
> >
> > - individual teachers
> >
> > - the whole department

Why Bother Assessing?

Assessment can seem like a chore that gets in the way of the teaching process. It has been one of the major tasks associated with the National Curriculum. But teachers are good at making judgements about how well their pupils are doing. If in no other way, their vast experience in marking and moderating GCSE coursework provides ample evidence of teacher skills in the area of assessing. The successful Head of Department will want to build on this to create an effective, comprehensive and coherent assessment process that makes sense to pupils, teachers and parents and which can be relatively easily managed. Moreover, the process should be a fundamental part of the way in which the department assures quality. Department staff will need to be convinced of the value of assessment as a tool in their drive to maintain and improve standards.

The Head of Department can focus on 4 key areas:

- Knowing how well pupils are doing
- Knowing how well the department is doing
- Making use of examination data
- What to record and report.

We will look at the importance of each one of these in turn.

Knowing how well pupils are doing

Teachers want to know that the pupils they teach are making progress. Intuitively they make sound judgements about who is doing well and who isn't. On top of this there are a range of methods for gaining more precise information about aspects of pupils' work.

The most important task for the Head of Department is to ensure that the department has defined those elements of knowledge, understanding and skills which teachers want pupils to develop. Only if the department is clear about what it intends the pupils to learn can assessment begin to be meaningful and useful. Such a debate within the department will also help to provide a clear focus for teaching. We have discussed in some detail how a department might identify and note the key learning intentions in the section on planning.

However the department chooses to approach the issue, it is crucial that there is agreement about what pupils are intended to learn.

Once this is established the department has to decide how to assess whether or not the desired learning has taken place. Again there is a need for agreement. A range of common assessments will help to generate consistency and quality across the department. Methods used will need to suit the type of learning being assessed. For example, a straightforward test might be most appropriate to assess the acquisition of knowledge, a piece of extended writing to evaluate conceptual understanding and an investigation to assess skill development.

The key questions for the Head of Department are:

Have we identified the intended learning?

Have we established a common set of assessments which will provide us with evidence of pupils' progress in these key areas?

Is the range of assessments appropriate for their purpose?

Heads of Department must assure themselves that as time goes by a profile is being built up of each pupil's progress in key aspects of knowledge, understanding and skills.

Knowing how well your department is doing
Assessment, when well managed, tells you more than how individual pupils are doing. It can tell you how effective you are being both as a teacher and as a department.

The key questions for the Head of Department here are:

How effective are we being at delivering the intended learning?

What parts of our teaching do we need to modify to make us more effective?

Having carefully designed the methods of assessment to find out about individual pupil progress in key areas, you now have a wealth of data available to the department which provides information about the effectiveness of your teaching. Too often this data relies solely on individual teachers marking books when in fact it should be being used as a tool for department self-review.

Of course the sharing of this data across the department needs to be handled sensitively. After all you will, to some extent, be looking at the effectiveness of individual teachers. Nevertheless, if as we suggest, you are building within your department a spirit of openness, a willingness to enquire and reflect on practice and generally creating a climate of self review, then most difficulties can be overcome.

Strategies for looking at the assessment data might look something like this:

- start small
- keep it collaborative as much as possible
- construct mark schemes for key assessments
- focus on sharing good practice
- draw on the expertise gained from GCSE
- don't create more work - make use of existing meeting time
- build confidence in the process.

You can start by focusing on one particular assessment which all pupils will take in, say, year 7. The department needs to agree that all pupils will take the assessment at a similar time. A common mark scheme will help teachers to mark the work with consistency as will an agreed grading system, whether it be by National Curriculum levels or other numerical or letter grades. Whatever you choose it will be important that the mark scheme has a strong focus on the 'intended learning'. Our suggestion would be to agree a five point scale, either A-E or 1-5 in the first instance. Of course, if the department or school already has an agreed system then so much the better.

Once all teachers have marked their group's work, agree to bring a small sample from each group to the department meeting. The sample might include a range of pupil abilities.

Issues to be discussed are:

- What is the range and quality of responses?
- Are there any particularly good or weak examples?
- Can we identify any reasons for differences in quality?
- Do we appear to be delivering the intended learning?
- Do we appear to be assessing reasonably consistently?

This kind of activity clearly has many benefits. Remember that an important purpose is to share good practice and encourage reflection. Two key outcomes from such a session could be:

- beginning to build up a department collection or portfolio of 'model' or exemplar responses
- the identification of teaching strategies which make a positive contribution to good quality responses.

It is not difficult to see how this kind of approach to assessment can begin to feed into the overall effectiveness of the department. You are now ready to take the process one step further.

Once your department feels comfortable with sharing the outcomes of assessment and can see the value of using assessment data in this way you can begin to use a larger quantity of the data more systematically. There are two key questions for the Head of Department:

- What kind of analysis should I expect class teachers to be undertaking?

✎ What data collection and analysis should I be doing centrally?

Having identified what pupils are expected to know, understand and be able to do, the assessments a class undertakes should provide teachers and the department with sound evidence of how effective a teaching programme has been. For example it might be that having completed a particular unit the assessments reveal that there were some aspects of the intended learning that very few pupils managed to grasp. This in all probability indicates that there is a need to adjust the teaching programme to ensure that these important features are covered more effectively. A systematic approach to making assessment work for you can be a powerful key element of a department's self-review process.

The effective Head of Department will be gathering assessment data centrally. The results of those assessments which have been agreed and are taken commonly by all children in each year group should be centrally logged (see example on page 27). This could be by class or, perhaps less threateningly, on a year group list. A department computer, if there is such a thing, is obviously the best method.

This has two important advantages for the Head of Department:

1. The progress of all pupils in key areas of knowledge, understanding and skills can be seen at a glance.

2. The success of the department in delivering its intended learning can be assessed including the identification of any particular areas of weakness which may need attention.

Making Use Of Examination Data
The analysis and interpretation of examination data has become an industry in its own right in recent times. Several agencies have sprung up which, at a price, will provide schools with data analysis services. In addition several Local Education Authorities provide their schools with 'value-added' data which provides important information indicating how well they have done, in terms of examinations, with their pupils, once intake data and socio-economic factors are taken into account. Given all this, how can the Head of Department use examination data to make the department more effective? (See example on page 28.)

There are 4 key types of data to explore:

● Predictive grades
● Actual examination grades
● Moderators' reports
● Examination data trends

The Head of Department needs to find answers to the following three questions from the data:

✎ What does this tell me about the performance of individual pupils?
✎ What does this tell me about the performance of individual teachers?
✎ What does this tell me about the performance of the department?

Central Assessment Log

Year/Tutor Group _____

Pupil's Name	Tutor Group	Class Teacher	Assessment 1	Assessment 2	Assessment 3	Assessment 4	Assessment 5	End of Year Assessment

Examination Data Log

Pupil's Name	Tutor Group	Teacher	End of Year 9 Grade	Year 10 Grade	Predicated Exam Grade	Actual Exam Grade	Comment

If the school has a climate in which this kind of data is shared and discussed openly then so much the better. Clearly the important issue to explore regarding individual pupils is whether they are performing in your subject appropriately for their ability. Three key issues are:

●   Is performance in line with prior achievement data?
●   Are any pupils not living up to that?
●   Are any over-achieving? (value added)

Heads of Department and subject teachers will bring to this process their own accumulated knowledge of individual children's ability. In addition this process can be assisted by seeing how they are performing in other similar or related subject areas.

For example, if a pupil in history has a predictive grade of 'E' and yet in English and Geography she has predictive grades of 'C' there is good reason to ask questions about under-performance. If analysis reveals a cluster of such possible under-performances in particular teaching groups, questions might be whether the expectations of particular teachers are appropriate, or indeed whether expectations within the department as a whole are too low. Equally, analysis could reveal areas where expectations are high and an exploration of this could be rewarding.

The same kind of analysis can and should be undertaken with actual examination grades. The value of looking closely at predictive grades is of course that there is still time to act on that analysis to influence the outcomes for the pupils concerned!

The examination board's moderator's report is a further useful piece of evidence. Its detailing of candidates' performance on the different components within the exam is another pointer to the relative strengths and weaknesses in the department's teaching.

The Head of Department needs to ask:

What does this tell us we are doing well?

What aspects of our practice do we need to refine?

When looking at any examination data it is important to bear in mind the long term view. We all know that performances can vary enormously from one year to the next. Some cohorts of pupils in a subject can contain a disproportionately large or small number of bright pupils. The staffing situation in a department in a particular year could be problematic. These things can influence results significantly. The questions for the Head of Department should be:

✎   How have we done over the last 3 to 5 years?
✎   Is the trend generally towards higher or lower performance?
✎   Can I identify and explain the factors influencing the trend?
✎   Given the abilities of the pupils, what should our target for performance be for the next 2 to 3 years?

Sample report

Pupil's Name	Year Group	Tutor Group	Subject	Teacher
Stephen Richards	**8**	**8TZ**	History	**Mrs H. Harris**

In history this year most work has founded on British history from 1500 to 1700. Throughout this work Stephen has shown a positive attitude to the topic. He has completed most of the homeworks to a good standard. His knowledge of the period is sound and he knows most of the key dates and events. He understands the reasons for the dispute between the monarchy and parliament and has developed his own point of view about the issue. He has shown himself able to use a variety of historical sources to investigate aspects of the period. I am pleased with his progress.

H Harris

Mrs. H. Harris

What to Record and Report

The issue of what to record in terms of pupil work and their progress has become both confusing and irritating. A lack of clarity has surrounded the area since the beginning of the National Curriculum.

Essentially the Head of Department must ask themselves:

What do we need to know about our pupils?
What is the most effective way to record the information?
(See example on page 30.)

A key factor here is that schools are legally obliged to report on pupils' progress annually in all subjects and some subjects of course need to report attainment in National Curriculum levels, at least at the end of a Key Stage. This implies that subjects must make sure that they record what pupils know, understand and can do with in terms of the key features of the National Curriculum.

To make this manageable, the department should identify a point possibly once or twice each term when key assessments take place. These assessments should relate specifically to particular key elements of the National Curriculum and possibly to aspects of the attainment targets. The results of these assessments over time will develop into a useful profile of pupils' abilities in the important aspects of the subject. These profiles will in turn, enable:

✎   the writing of quality reports for parents which contain information on pupils subject-related strengths and areas which need development.

✎   the making of informed judgements to assign individual pupils to levels within attainment targets if necessary.

The Head of Department, wanting to make the best use of this data will, as discussed above, want to create a way of logging the data from such assessments centrally.

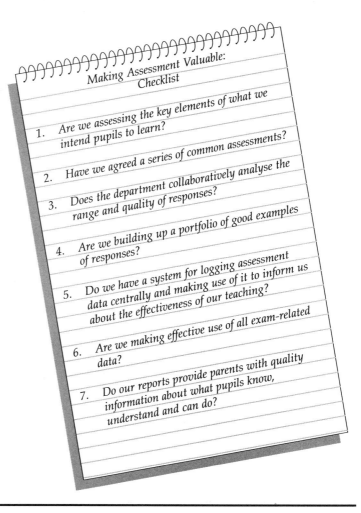

Making Assessment Valuable: Checklist

1. Are we assessing the key elements of what we intend pupils to learn?

2. Have we agreed a series of common assessments?

3. Does the department collaboratively analyse the range and quality of responses?

4. Are we building up a portfolio of good examples of responses?

5. Do we have a system for logging assessment data centrally and making use of it to inform us about the effectiveness of our teaching?

6. Are we making effective use of all exam-related data?

7. Do our reports provide parents with quality information about what pupils know, understand and can do?

Section Three

Managing Departmental Resources

> **In Section Three you will learn that:**
>
> ☞ **Department staff need:**
>
> - clear guidance and expectations
> - access to professional development
> - identified strengths and skills
> - quality time
>
> ☞ **Finance needs planning and recording**
>
> ☞ **Resources for learning should be considered in terms of**
>
> - cost
> - access
> - quality
>
> ☞ **Resources outside the department must be accessed.**

What are a department's resources?

There is a tendency to think about resources as texts, worksheets, IT equipment and so on. Here we are considering resources in a wider sense, including:

- Department Staff
- Finance
- Resources for Learning
- Resources outside the department

Resources are vital components of successful teaching and the effective Head of Department will want to make the most of what is available.

Department Staff

These are clearly the department's most valuable resource. Whenever appointments can be made, the school and Head of Department will strive to appoint teachers who have appropriate expertise and the motivational abilities to inspire young people. Once appointed, it is the job of the Head of Department to provide the opportunities and support to enable the teacher to function as effectively as possible. What form should this support take? There are 4 key elements:

Clear guidance and expectations

Staff need to know what is expected of them. This is primarily true in terms of what staff are expected to teach, hence the need for clear and helpful schemes of work. It is also the case in terms of issues like assessment, marking, equality of opportunity and all those issues for which a department statement of policy is helpful. The potential usefulness of departmental documentation is discussed in more detail in Section One.

We cannot assume that somehow staff, no matter how experienced, will automatically do things in the way in which you, as Head of Department want them to be done. The same is true of department expectations of classroom routines, the quality of the classroom environment and behaviour. Being clear about all these issues and the contributions staff are expected to make will contribute significantly to the effectiveness of the department.

Access to professional development

The good Head of Department will want their staff to develop professionally. This is good for the department and the member of staff. In these difficult financial times opportunities are often limited. Nevertheless staff need to feel that they are supported and encouraged by their Head of Department when appropriate opportunities arise. It can be helpful for the department to establish criteria for accessing professional development to ensure a sense of fairness and no doubt these will, to a large degree, mirror those of the whole school. An important consideration will be that any such development is a good fit with the contents and targets contained in the departmental development plan. A department team which keeps up to date with developments in their subject and in education in general will be one which maintains morale and self-confidence.

Key criteria for accessing professional development:

1. **Course or activity content is in line with targets in School Development Plan.**

2. **Course or activity is in line with targets in Department Development Plan.**

3. **Course or activity will support the individual teachers own professional and career development and will enhance the skills and expertise within the department.**

Part of professional development is enabling staff to make contributions to the thinking of the department and to take on responsibilities wherever this is appropriate. It is hard to overstate the positive impact an effective Head of Department can have in this respect. Staff can be enabled to make contributions in a variety of situations from input to department meetings to leading aspects of curriculum development. Responsibilities might be offered or encouraged with regard to year or Key Stage co-ordination or perhaps reviewing aspects of practice. Of course not all staff want such opportunities but the Head of Department should look to provide them wherever there is fertile ground.

Appropriate use of skills

Much of this is related to the section on professional development but there are other things to consider. A Head of Department should know the strengths, skills and talents of his/her staff. This may, for example, be to do with specific aspects of the subject, skills with particular age groups of pupils or maybe some cross- curricular expertise. How many departments contain a 'secret' expert in IT who could be used to skill up other members of the team and so improve the provision of IT within the dept. How about the Geography teacher who made a special study at university of the causes and effects of earthquakes but who has not been invited to make a contribution to that aspect of the Key Stage 3 curriculum! Know your staff and use them to best effect.

Quality time

In the hurly-burly of life in a secondary school, it is sometimes hard to find time for anything other than a snatched conversation while walking from one lesson to another or at best it might be a quick chat over a cup of coffee in the staff room. The good Head of Department will realise that the staff will value and benefit from a professional discussion about their work and the work of the department as regularly as one can be afforded. Such a meeting is more than an informal discussion. There may well be an agenda for such sessions, jointly constructed between the Head of Department and the individual member of staff. It is important to note that these sessions should not be seen as appraisal but rather a means of providing support and an opportunity for a professional discussion in an atmosphere of relative calm. With a little organisation (as well as a bit of luck) it is usually possible to offer one such discussion per year. Even if it can't be arranged on the timetable, most teachers would be happy to give up a little time either at lunchtime or after school for this activity. The benefits can be substantial. For the Head of Department it's a good opportunity to give praise, be positive, raise morale and explore how to develop staff further. It can also provide useful feedback on how people feel about the way the department is being managed!

Professional Development Discussion with
Dave Roberts
Tuesday 16th September 11.30 am

Agenda

1. New timetable / groups

2. Last summer's exam results

3. This year's professional development   - courses
*   - in-house*

4. Department Development Plan - any issues

5. Any other business

Finance

If any resource is scarce it's this one. When financial restrictions are great there is no better time to ensure efficient and effective financial management. It can be tempting to say that as there isn't much money anyway, there is little point in putting much effort into this aspect of the department's resources. However, for the department that wants to develop, making the most of a little is vital. The following list of key questions will help those wishing to tighten their financial processes:

✎ **Do you keep a record of actual spending as you go through the year?**

Building up a year by year record, in a form which allows for easy comparisons to be made, can help in making a more accurate forecast for coming years and will provide accurate and useful evidence on which to base decisions about reducing or increasing spending. You should include all spending, no matter how small or how unusual. (See example on page 37.)

✎ **Is financial planning securely linked to the department's development plan?**

It is possible to cost almost all the targets contained in your development plan. Some items might be relatively straightforward such as the purchase of a new set of texts to resource a new exam or unit of work. Other less tangible items, such as professional development, can also be costed in terms of estimated course fees or supply cover costs. Some development items will need to be funded over several years. For example, a history department might wish to accumulate its own collection of replica artefacts. It would be hard to achieve this all at once but the allocation of a small amount of funds over several years can be very effective. As with all developments, if financial planning is careful, the development is more likely to succeed.

✎ **Do you have a view of future maintenance and replacement costs for key items of equipment?**

Increasingly many departments use equipment which needs regular maintenance or which needs replacing either because of wear and tear or because it has become obsolete. The most obvious example of this is computer hardware which as technology develops, presents schools with major financial difficulties in their attempt to keep up. There are plenty of other examples too, often in science and technology departments. The prudent Head of Department will attempt to forecast these major aspects of future spending, if only to alert the school to the financial implications.

Resources for learning

This is of course the main area where heads of department can make spending decisions. The key areas to consider are:

- purchase.
- access.
- monitoring quality.

Department Spending Year on Year

Item	1994	1995	1996	1997
Exercise Books				
File Paper				
Pens / Pencils				
Folders				
Field Work Support				
I.T. Hardware				
I.T. Software				
Televisions				
Video Tapes				
Maintenance Costs				

Purchase

The important factor here is value for money. This is best achieved when there is a good fit between the needs of the department, the quality of the resource and the cost.

A sound purchasing strategy might contain the following features:

- Do the resources fit well with our schemes of work?
- Can the resource be readily used in the way we want to use it?
- How will the resource support or enhance our range of teaching and learning styles?
- Am I sure the resource is appropriate for the intended age and ability group?
- Have I assembled a range of alternative resources to enable comparisons to be made?
- Is there good guidance about how to get the best out of the resource?
- Is the resource sufficiently durable?
- Does the resource have any equality of opportunity implications?
- Have I sought the opinions of other department staff about the resource?

When you can answer these questions positively you can be reasonably certain that your money is being spent wisely.

Access

Having accumulated good resources you want to make sure that the department gets the best out of them. This really hinges around good organisation and good housekeeping. A cluttered stock room, disordered filing cabinets and untidy shelves do not assist effective resource management. Staff need to know what the department has available and where to locate it. Resources being in the right place at the right time increase efficiency and reduce stress. This well-ordered and careful approach also increases the lifespan of your resources. The following simple rules will help:

- Make sure there is an up to date inventory of all the resources the department has.
- Insist on good resource management routines from all staff, e.g. resources need to be returned to the appropriate place after use.
- Larger resources (TV, Video) may need a booking and signing-out system.
- Storage systems need clear labelling, to be understood by all staff and their organisation needs regular monitoring to ensure they remain effective.

In large departments in particular it can be useful if responsibility for resource oversight for each year group or each key stage can be delegated to different members of staff. This can share the load as well as drawing other staff into an important aspect of management.

Monitoring quality

Even in the most effectively managed department, the quality of resources can deteriorate over time. Day to day wear and tear takes its toll but other factors will also influence the situation. Some issues to consider include:

- The rate of loss of texts and other resources.
- The appropriateness of the resources as courses change.

✎ The appropriateness of language and images as society changes - in particular with regard to sexual or racial stereotyping.

Effective resource management implies keeping these issues under regular review to ensure that quality is maintained.

Resources outside the department

Most departments have access to resources other than their own and the skilled use of these can significantly enhance the quality of educational provision. The most fruitful of these are usually the Special Educational Needs Department, the school's IT provision and the library.

Special Educational Needs Department

The skills which reside with the staff in such a department are often underused. The Head of Department who wants to pursue strategies for differentiation and who wishes to make the work of the department more accessible to pupils can profit from close links with staff. This isn't just about getting them to design a worksheet. It is more about seeking advice that will inform the department's teaching and learning styles as well as making print based resources more appropriate. They could well feed in at some appropriate point to the curriculum design process, or perhaps visit department meetings. How many Heads of Department consult with SEN staff when making significant purchases of texts? These teachers often have great skill in the area of readability.

Many schools use in class support as part of their Special Needs Provision. Support staff can be teachers or non-teaching classroom assistants. There has to be effective, two way liaison if this support is to be used to its best advantage.

Areas for liaison might include:

- clear understanding of the learning needs of the supported pupils
- providing details of schemes of work/lesson plans to support staff in advance of lessons
- utilising support staff to ensure pupils are clear about tasks and instructions (classwork, homework, deadlines, length etc.)
- evaluation of legibility/readability of resources

Other issues will emerge as the support becomes established. The important point is that all those involved in providing/receiving/deploying support need to plan and collaborate to ensure its potential to enhance learning is fully realised.

The school's IT provision

Many departments still have generally low levels of IT provision for their pupils. This can be due to a variety of factors including a lack of competence and confidence on the part of staff, little access to computer hardware and lack of finance to purchase relevant software. These are all significant difficulties but the Head of Department who is determined to improve provision may well be able to work with staff with responsibility for IT to:

✎ get time for staff to use machines.
✎ tailor a course to develop staff skills.
✎ work with department staff and their teaching groups.
✎ locate or develop pieces of software appropriate for the subject.

Each of these go some way towards positively developing the department's approach to IT.

The library

The library and librarian constitute one of the most extensive resources for learning in the school and departments need to make the best use of them. When the links between department and library are strong the resource provision for pupils is enhanced. This is not just a matter of letting pupils use the library. As ever, good planning pays dividends and opportunities to work with the librarian need to be created. The more they know about what you teach and when you teach it, the more they are likely to have resources available to support your curriculum. Questions to consider include:

- does the librarian have a scheduled copy of our schemes of work?
- do I invite them to department meetings when resources are being discussed?
- do I discuss regularly with the librarian the kinds of resources which would enhance learning in my subject? These could be texts, IT, CD ROM.
- do I liaise with the libriarian to ensure displays of relevant resources are available when we teach a topic?

Most librarians would welcome the opportunity to be more involved in curriculum planning and many have a great deal of knowledge and expertise to offer. The effect on the quality of the curriculum is positive.

Managing Departmental Resources: Checklist

1. Is there clear guidance for staff with regard to all key aspects of performance?

2. Are staff encouraged to undertake professional development?

3. Am I making the best use of staff expertise?

4. Do I offer department staff quality time to discuss issues with me?

5. Am I keeping a detailed record of department spending?

6. Have I linked costs to development plan targets?

7. Have I considered future high cost replacement and maintenance issues?

8. Have I got a clearly stated purchasing strategy?

9. Is access to resources for learning effective?

10. Do I have a system for regularly reviewing the quality of department resources?

11. Have I established effective links with SEN, IT and library staff?

Developing the link between Heads of Department & Senior Managers

In Section Four you will learn that:

☞ *Links with Senior Managers are essential for:*
- *development planning*
- *achievement analysis*
- *staffing and resources*

☞ *Meetings with senior staff should be:*
- *frequent*
- *manageable*
- *involving*

Much is expected of the Head of Department today. The role has never been more important. As the need to deliver good test and examination results increases in order to maintain or improve the school's position in the league tables, so does the pressure. But the Head of Department cannot do the job alone. He or she has a right to the support of their Senior Managers and that support needs to be active rather than passive. In turn, the Senior Management Team have legitimate expectations of their Heads of Department. This chapter briefly explores how the links between the two groups might be made more effective.

Much of this section is focused on what the Senior Management Team might reasonably expect of an effective Head of Department. These characteristics could be summarised as:

✎ the provision of good leadership.
✎ ensuring sound planning, effective teaching and secure assessment.
✎ managing resources effectively.
✎ developing a strong department team.
✎ making sound links with the community.

These are high expectations and cannot be achieved without support. It is no longer good enough for the only substantial link between the Head of Department and the Senior Management Team to be the annual meeting sometime in September which is an exam results post mortem - pat on the back if the results are good and do better next time if they're not.

The delivery of high expectations requires a real investment in quality time from both parties. In essence there is a need for more regular formal contact. Of course Heads of Department and members of the Senior Management Team will often talk informally about a variety of issues but this is insufficient to deliver the quality linkage which will develop effective department management. A major benefit for the Senior Management Team, if the suggested model is adopted, is the development of a much better knowledge of the school, its workings and of course its strengths and weaknesses. Time is precious and some might say that there are already too many meetings to attend. We would argue that meetings of this nature have the potential to deliver such enormous benefits that a school should strive to give them a high degree of priority.

What are the purposes of the link?

3 key issues can be identified:

- Development planning
- Achievement analysis
- Staffing and resource issues

In essence these 3 issues should form the basis of a rolling agenda. It is an agenda which can and should contain elements of support and challenge for both the Head of Department and the members of the Senior Management Team.

Development Planning

Most Heads of Department are now expected to produce a development plan, sometimes annually, sometimes every two or three years but with annual reviews and updates. Sadly these plans, once complete, often fade from view. This is a great pity when often considerable thought has gone into their construction. The Head of Department/SMT link meeting is an opportunity to keep the development plan alive. Relevant questions to be explored would be:

- what progress is being made with each target?
- are timescales being adhered to?
- what particular achievements need to be noted?
- what difficulties have been encountered?
- what support needs have emerged?
- how can the Senior Management Team help?

Achievement analysis

Raising achievement has never been as prominent an issue as it is today, and there is more to achievement than GCSE and A Level examination results. Equally the Senior Management Team needs to have a broad understanding of standards of achievement in departments. In this context, the link meeting provides an opportunity for the following issues to be discussed:

- what systems are in place to assess and record achievement?
- what does the data tell us about standards in particular year groups?
- are these standards appropriate, given what we know of pupils' abilities?
- are there any individual classes, year groups, or courses where standards are low?
- what reasons can be identified to explain any difficulties?
- what action needs to be taken?
- how can the Senior Management Team help?

Staffing and resource issues

Obviously these are likely to form part of the discussions relating to the other items but there is some merit in giving them an agenda slot in their own right. Much of the skill of being an effective Head of Department is related to getting the best out of people and other resources. The Senior Management Team need an up-to-date awareness of the department's strengths and weaknesses in these important areas. Equally a Head of Department needs to know that they have the understanding and support of the Senior Management Team when difficulties arise. The head of department needs someone with whom they can discuss such things calmly and constructively. Key points in the discussion would be:

- Is the quantity and quality of resources adequate to deliver the courses?
- Where and what are the shortcomings?
- Are there any staffing issues, positive or negative, we need to discuss?
- What strategies can we put in place to improve those situations about which there are concerns?

It is not difficult to see how these professional discussions can produce a more informed Senior Management Team and a better supported Head of Department. They can be a vital factor in the school's drive to maintain and improve standards and to monitor quality. So if we agree that such links are worthwhile, some key questions remain to be answered:

- How often should these meetings take place?
- Who from the Senior Management Team should be involved?
- Does the linkage extend to anything other than meetings?

Meeting frequency

To produce any reasonable level of continuity of knowledge and support such meetings need to take place more than just annually. Our suggestion would be that provision needs to be made for a meeting each term as standard practice. There may, in some cases, be a need for more frequent meetings as particular issues arise. We also believe that some kind of written record, however brief, needs to be maintained, indicating any decisions reached or targets agreed.

Senior Management Team representation

Clearly this role is too large for only the Head to be involved. The most effective strategy is for each member of the Senior Management Team to assume the link role with a small number of departments or faculties. In most schools this will probably mean each of the Senior Management Team member becoming involved with 3 or 4 departments. This should be manageable in the school which recognises the potential benefits.

Involvement other than meetings

The intention of developing this linkage is that the member of the Senior Management Team develops extensive knowledge and understanding of the department. Equally, from the point of view of the Head of Department, the Senior Management Team member is to some extent 'their person'. Therefore there may well be a wider range of involvements. These could include:

- rota arrangements for attending department meetings.
- oversight of department reports to parents.

Effective Heads of Department

✎ attendance at any curriculum evenings for parents or governors.

✎ accompanying the department on field trips.

Essentially the role of the Senior Management Team member in this context becomes that of critical friend. They should be supportive and encouraging, always endeavouring to maintain and raise morale by providing positive feedback whenever possible. In addition, the role expects that challenge will be made whenever performance or quality falls below expectations.

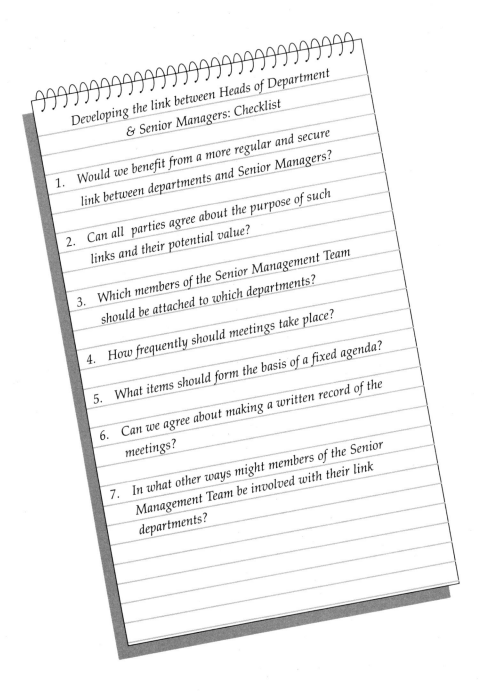

Developing the link between Heads of Department & Senior Managers: Checklist

1. Would we benefit from a more regular and secure link between departments and Senior Managers?

2. Can all parties agree about the purpose of such links and their potential value?

3. Which members of the Senior Management Team should be attached to which departments?

4. How frequently should meetings take place?

5. What items should form the basis of a fixed agenda?

6. Can we agree about making a written record of the meetings?

7. In what other ways might members of the Senior Management Team be involved with their link departments?

Leadership

In Section Five you will learn that department leadership includes:

- ☛ **Providing a vision and sense of purpose**
- ☛ **Setting quality standards**
- ☛ **Monitoring effectiveness**
- ☛ **Creating the right culture**
- ☛ **Planning**
- ☛ **Professional development**
- ☛ **Rewarding achievement**
- ☛ **Providing a role model**

Many (perhaps most) people possess the ability to acquire a range of skills and learn strategies which can make them effective leaders. Leadership style may be a function of innate personality but leadership effectiveness is a variable which can be enhanced by progressively learning to do important things in effective ways.

This section outlines the most vital activities in providing effective leadership.

Providing a vision and sense of purpose

DEPARTMENTAL SACRED COWS & HISTORICAL PRECEDENTS

Creating a vision for the future development of a department is an important and essentially collaborative activity. This, of necessity, will involve dialogue right across the team and will include critical examination of existing assumptions, 'sacred cows' and historical precedents. Effective teams not only tolerate the differences of opinion which occur in such discussions, they build upon their differences to create new understanding. Eventually aims, wish lists and targets are formulated into shared ambitions. The most vital activity is the linked creation of a shared sense of purpose to work towards all agreed goals. In this it needs to be remembered that ownership of the creation of a new policy is less significant than its implementation, even if in many cases, those two factors are inextricably linked.

The following example resulted from a staff development aims and objectives exercise during which the departmental team were asked to identify 10 key aims. The exercise produced aims covering the following areas:

1. The Curriculum - content
2. The Curriculum - updating
3. The Curriculum - design of materials
4. The Curriculum - teaching methods
5. Pupil A

6.   Pupil Attitudes
7.   Resource Management
8.   Departmental Organisation
9.   Staff Development
10. Public Relations

For each of the 10 aims the team brainstormed 10 objectives, resulting in a shared vision of the department's purpose. This example is taken from the document that developed out of this activity:

Aim 6.

Pupil Attitudes

Pupils are encouraged to develop self-control, self-reliance, initiative, positive feelings towards their work and a desire to extend their study beyond the classroom.

6.1   Classrooms are arranged and resources designed so that pupils take maximum responsibility for resource distribution and retrieval.

6.2   Expectations about pupils taking responsibility for their own actions and learning are frequently communicated.

6.3   Pupils who fail to bring essential equipment listed in their 'Guide to Science' are required to copy out the list of essential equipment.

6.4   Resource materials are colour coded and boxed so that they are easy to operate under the supervision of substitute teachers unfamiliar with the system.

6.5   Pupils who fail to fulfil the '13 Pupils' Expectations' displayed in each tutor base are given extra training and relevant remedial tasks.

6.6   Homework and projects are set which require pupils, independently, to gather data, do experiments and organise their data into conclusions over a period of several days or weeks.

6.7   Every effort is made to motivate pupils by giving them the experience of success in and praise for work done.

6.8   Ego-involving activities are included in units, as is active group work such as simulations and field trips which provide enjoyment as well as learning.

6.9   Wherever possible, pupils are given scope to follow up their particular interests or make their own choices within the framework of the course.

6.10 Pupil work is put forward for publication in the school magazine.

Prerequisites

- A consistent wish to improve the provision made for children.
- A willingness to use shared future ambitions to determine current activity.

Setting and pursuing quality standards

Managers play a central role in establishing the expectations of their team, whether that is establishing the expectations outsiders have of the team or the expectations which team members have of themselves. Constantly and consistently restating the characteristics of high level performance is as important with groups of teachers as it is with groups of children. In an ideal world the articulation of the success criteria is sufficient to ensure high levels of achievement. The effective middle manager, however, realises the need for wider 'vocabulary' of strategies and uses a range of tactics from positive reinforcement of existing achievement through direct professional challenge of inadequate work.

Taken from the same staff development example used previously, this checklist covers the need to keep the content current.

Aim 2.

The Curriculum - updating
Staff ensure that curriculum content and approach includes current developments in subject disciplines and contemporary issues.

2.1   All staff read and discuss subject periodicals.
2.2   The department library is regularly replenished with current publications, both books and periodicals.
2.3   A current affairs noticeboard accessible to pupils is kept up-to-date, including publicity about current relevant TV and radio programmes.
2.4   Video recordings of current transmissions are used with classes to stimulate their interest in current affairs.
2.5   Pupils are encouraged to bring in news articles and to discuss news items - relating them to the course.
2.6   Pupils are encouraged to write about current topics for publication in the school magazine or community newspaper.
2.7   Year co-ordinators review courses annually to identify and remedy obsolescent content or method.
2.8   Team members attend in-service courses to keep abreast of current developments in their subject areas and in teaching methods.
2.9   County Science Advisers or university personnel are invited to department in-service meetings or days to conduct seminars to stimulate monitoring and development of the course.
2.10   Team members provide in-service sessions to colleagues in other schools in order to acquire a perspective on the up-to-dateness of their courses and methods.

Key areas in which middle managers should establish agreed and pursued notions of quality include:

- ✎   the regularity and rigour of marking.
- ✎   the thoroughness of teacher planning.
- ✎   the provision and pursuit of homework.
- ✎   the provision for variety of learning.
- ✎   the creation of challenging teaching.
- ✎   communication with parents.
- ✎   the setting of achievement targets for external and internal assessments.

Prerequisites:

- ● A well developed education philosophy and set of values.
- ● The ability to translate those into quite precise (not necessarily quantified but preferably assessable) goals.

We will know our departmental assessment is successful if:-

- ● every exercise book is marked once per fornight

- ● every piece of marking includes advice on how the student can improve

- ● we make twice as many positive comments as negative ones

- ● we employ our grading system consistently

- ● students assess their own work at least once per month

- ● students set themselves new targets

Monitoring the effectiveness of the team

The word monitoring has increasingly acquired a series of negative dimensions in recent times, based largely upon ideas that the purposes of such activity are to expose poor performance, to adjust teachers' pay, or at worst, to provide evidence to dismiss teachers. Effective middle managers openly challenge such negative ideas and, by their words and actions, emphasise the gains to be made through monitoring. They seek to establish the view that monitoring provides real insight which indicates where learning is effective, informs planning, enables resources to be targeted, informs professional development and above all recognises and rewards achievement. Section seven of this book covers monitoring and evaluation in more detail.

Prerequisites:

- A working knowledge of practical monitoring strategies, particularly classroom observation, pupil work, analysis of examination results, (preferably on a value added basis) and, most importantly self review techniques which the team can use.

The following model of classroom observation developed from the work of Joyce and Showers on Effective Staff Development is particularly helpful in developing an open climate within a department. Used sensitively with an agenda set by the person being observed, rather than the person doing the observation, it leads into a process of self-review which can be none threatening.

Four Stages in Lesson Observation

| Pre-Lesson Discussion | When? Where? |
| Observer ←→ Teacher | How? What to observe? |

| Observation | Passive observer role. |
| Observer ⟶ Teacher | Descriptive note-taking. |

| Separate Reflection | Examine notes. |
| Observer ‖ Teacher | Identify questions and issues to discuss. |

| Post-Lesson Discussion | What happened? Could it be improved? |
| Observer ←→ Teacher | How? Next observation? |

Creating and maintaining a departmental 'culture'

Effective teams have a kind of 'culture' of reflection which routinely includes structured review and evaluation of their work. Professional challenge is accepted as part of normal working relationships. That professional challenge is not compromised within the team because it is understood by all to be distinct from and separate from interpersonal relationships. Teams which have such characteristics as a spirit of enquiry, a collective willingness to problem solve, an ability to accept change as the natural order and build upon it are usually more successful. Teams which routinely share and exchange examples of good practice (lesson plans, worksheets etc.) are nearly always more successful and frequently save each other much hard work. Teams which have a 'culture' where teaching and learning are consistently recognised as the vital activities and other activities are minimised are the most successful of all.

Prerequisites:

- A willingness to openly and critically review one's own beliefs.
- A recognition that the achievement team culture of the team is significant in determining progress.

Planning

Long before DES, DEF or the DFEE published documentation extolling the virtues of management development and action planning, teams of teacher were collaborating to produce plans to guide their day-to-day lessons, their termly schemes of work and their long term developments. Planning is the device by which we focus our efforts on the important and protect ourselves from the less significant. An effective Head of Department is likely to be someone who ensures her/his team plans both short and long term, are thoroughly prepared, used and reviewed, and does not allow that team to simply exist by reacting to day-to-day crises.

Prerequisite:

- A knowledge of different planning and a willingness to 'helicopter' above everyday events, keeping sight of the big issues.

Facilitating professional development

Every professional has a duty to themselves to evaluate their own professional development needs, articulating them through channels provided by the department or the school. A good Head of Department will ensure those channels are well established and in turn well used by the team members.

Here again is the result of the aims and objectives exercise as it related to staff development:

Aim 9.

Staff Development

Team members engage in a continuous, systematic process of developing their ability to design, implement and evaluate learning activities.

9.1   Resources designed by team members are always submitted for constructive criticism by colleagues and the Design Co-Ordinator.

9.2   All team members take part in the design of work.

9.3   The Special Needs Co-Ordinator trains team members in skills required to design and implement resources for pupils with learning difficulties.

9.4   The Enrichment Co-Ordinator provides training in techniques for teaching gifted pupils.

9.5   The Design Co-Ordinator provides training in resource design skills.

9.6   The Head of Department develops a systematic programme of department focused in-service training.

9.7   The Head of Department encourages team members to attend appropriate external courses.

9.8   Subject specialists instruct colleagues in the latest developments in specialist disciplines.

9.9   The Head of Department provides individual counselling and careers advice to team members.

9.10   The Head of Department organises mutual observation and analysis of lessons to develop class management skills.

They should not depend upon the assertiveness of the individual. They should be fed by regular reviews (sometimes collective but usually individual, personal meetings) between the Head of Department and the team member.

Memo

Personal Meeting

To: All members of Department
FROM: Head of Department

Now that Yr 11 &13 have finished their exams and departed, I would like to have my full annual review with each of you. I know we will have our big, collective meeting next week but I am also interested in your individual views, particularly so that I can try to ensure the right INSET training & development opportunities are provided.

Suggested Agenda:

1. The year's successes & achievements (yours in particular)
2. Aspects which you are disappointed about (please refer to your monitoring/self review sheets)
3. Your development needs (NB new A level syllabus)
4. Your changing role in the department
5. Our aims/plans for the next year

I will contact you shortly to arrange a suitable time.

These meetings should also be based upon real information gathered from monitoring and evaluation and not just on the opinions of these involved. They should anticipate the future developments of the department and the individual, perhaps in the light of changed syllabi.

It is clear that not all middle managers see themselves in the role of leading practitioner of their team yet it is clear that most team managers wish for leadership in the form of advice and support about their teaching.

Ultimately a Head of Department's ability to enhance the professional development of colleagues depends on accepting the requirement to provide continuing leadership; knowledge of each team member's perception of his/her own professional development needs and an understanding insight into those needs arising from classroom observation.

Rewarding Achievement

Effective leaders can be ruthless in recognising and applanding positive achievements. Be wary, however, of falling into the trap of bland positivism, praising every task regardless of value, and tempering praise with challenges to unacceptable work. Aim to create a sense of purpose by a use of individual and collective praise which leaves team members with a sense of worth arising from the success gained.

Prerequisite:

- The ability to recognise the positive and the difficult. Ultimately the ability to create a collective feel-good factor will depend on real knowledge about teachers' and pupils' work.

Providing a strong personal, professional role model

Setting a professional example to other teachers is an often stated but rarely scrutinised way of providing leadership. It is sometimes interpreted narrowly, based upon the belief that it is rather difficult for a team leader to persuade someone to do something unless that team leader has shown willingness to do that job themselves. Phrases like *'Being willing to get your feet wet'* and *'Being in the front line with the troops'* are often quoted by Heads of Department. It is clear, however, that setting an example takes on many other dimensions. Professional example should provide a range of signals to colleagues. These might include routine exemplars of how thoroughly a function (e.g. report writing) should be carried out. Also guidance, by example, on how to deal with a difficult, disruptive child or how to handle, assertively, an unreasonable request is an important aspect of leadership.

It is a well recognised finding that two value systems cannot exist in one organisation. It follows from this that where the Head of Department has high expectations of how the staff should relate to pupils, the Head of Department should relate to the departmental team in the same vain. Consistency is all important in matters of:

- Praise
- High Challenge
- Low stress
- Support
- Self-reliance
- Openess
- Clarity of expectations
- Fun

Prerequisite:

- A recognition that the key issue in setting an example to colleagues is not usually persuading them to work harder but persuading them to work more effectively.

Effective Leadership: Checklist

1. Have you established a vision of where the department needs to go?

2. Have you translated that vision/goal into concrete actions that can be carried out by all?

3. Have you created quality expectations to work towards?

4. Are you consistently monitoring practice against agreed aims/expectations/and praising those who do meet aims?

5. Are you chivvying/harrying those who do not meet aims/expectations?

6. Are you identifying weaknesses and pursuing strategies to remedy them?

7. Are you planning and prioritising on the basis of clear values?

8. Are you minimising unimportant issues and concentrating upon the significant (not always the most urgent)?

9. Are you providing an effective role model?

Section Six

Making Links With The Community

In Section Six you will learn:

☞ **What constitutes effective links with parents**

☞ **How these links can be established through**
- *meetings*
- *marking*
- *homeworks*
- *explanations*

☞ **How to use the community for curriculum enhancement**

Although few adults in Britain would readily choose to sport an American style car bumper sticker saying 'My daughter is a high achiever at Rydal High', most parents and teachers in Britain would welcome closer links between schools and their community. It is not necessary to visit the schools of the USA, Denmark or Italy to visualise the gains which can emerge from parents, local commerce, industry and the community at large uniting in their support of their local school. Clearly a single Head of Department acting in isolation cannot shape the entire nature and effectiveness of those links. However it is possible for a single department, acting in unison, to bridge some of the gap that exists between teacher and most parents and thereby marshal support for the curriculum and pupil achievement.

Effective links with parents tend to be characterised by:

✎ early indicators about how a child is settling down in their new classroom. A timetable for reports could ensure that the parents of the intake year receive a report at the end of the first half term covering items such as attitudes to work; attitudes to homework; equipment required etc.

✎ regular communication in accessible language. Much of the knowledge we have about the design and layout of pupil resources is equally valid for communication to parents. Whilst words like 'aims' and 'objectives' are commonplace in the staffroom, they may not be amongst all parents. We need to think about our use of:
- specialist language
- line length
- inter-line spacing
- illustration
- headings
- bullets

in the literature we send to parents. Aim to make each communication as near as you can to the quality of your school prospectus.

✎ regular face to face contact (teacher with child and parents). Making sure that communication is about good work and behaviour as well as poor work and behaviour. It is worth noting that for optimum performance we need four positive comments for every negative one.

✎ communication about good work and behaviour (in addition to any other communication).

✎ early communication of 'warning signals' before they become serious issues. Many schools have homework diaries. An additional space on each page for staff comments enables communication on a daily basis if necessary.

✎ rigorous and regular marking of book/folders. Routines can be established whereby targets are identified through marking and parents are requested to initial in the margin that they have seen the targets.

✎ written information about homework set. Again establishing clear routines about completing homework diaries is important.

✎ early warning of visits and events.

✎ swift responses to questions and complaints. Heading a department is very demanding. Time invested in responding to issues swiftly can prevent matters escalating to the point at which they demand most of our time.

✎ a low limit on the number of 'begging' or 'fund-raising' letters. Avoid confusing or diluting your message. One single School Fund contribution is less antagonistic.

✎ explanations of policies followed. Schools which have actively pursued Accelerated Learning Techniques (see Book 1 in this series) have invited parents to evening training sessions which cover:

- whole brain learning
- multiple intelligences
- building self-esteem
- learning environments
- reducing learner stress

so they can help their children to be smarter.

✎ information which enables parents to fulfil an active support role (and validates that role). In this respect communication to parents which, when carefully written, have proved to be constructive and effective have included:

✎ help us to help your child.

✎ how to help your daughter/son with their homework.

✎ supporting your child in the build up to their examinations.

✎ recognising and dealing with stress in your child.

✎ if you are thinking of buying a computer... (advice on what might be most supportive of pupils' work in school).

✎ our marking and assessment policy.

✎ your child's coursework.

✎ books that might help your child.

✎ what to do if you are unhappy with your child's work.

✎ what you can reasonably expect from your child's teacher.

Clearly timing, frequency, language and sensitivity to the range of parental or carer circumstances must all be considered carefully. Tension between parents and school frequently arises due to the vacuum caused by lack of understanding and knowledge. An effective Head of Department can do much to minimise that vacuum by a judicious and informative range of communications.

Extract from Departmental Handbook
Year Co-ordinators

There will be one co-ordinator for each of years 7, 8 & 9 with two further co-ordinators for years 10 &11 after 1996.
The functions of the Year Co-ordinators are:

1. To arrange all A/V presentations for their year which involves:
    a checking with teachers that they are ready for presentation
    b. booking A/V materials
    c. Preparing the lecture theatre as necessary

2. To arrange all field trips for their year which involves:
    a. booking of coaches
    b. booking of venues as necessary
    c. preparation of letter informing parents of field trips.

    The letter should include the reason for the trip with a brief summary of the work involved, date and time of the trip, a list of equipment necessary for the trip, the cost per child and a slip for return with the money. The letter should always be typed, vetted by a member of the Senior Management and signed by the Head of Department.

    d. completion of Form SJ1 prior to the visit and SJ11 after the visit.

3. To monitor teaching within the year to see that the groups are progressing at the same pace.

4. To modify teachers' notes for the topics being taught in their year in the light of matters arising at Department Meetings.

With team teaching, the Year Co-ordinator's role is crucial to the smooth running of the department.

A second purpose in making links with the community can be for the purpose of curriculum enhancement. Often individual teachers make interesting and useful contacts in the community, but these are sometimes guarded jealously, when they could be shared amongst a wider group of students.

The enhancement itself can take a variety of forms including:

● Devices to include the community.

● Work awareness exercises which allow pupils to put their learning into a vocational context can be very useful in helping them to see the relevance of the curriculum in a working situation. Also such work experience opportunities, if carefully integrated and followed up, can often help with the complex process of making informed career decisions at some later stage. Although this would normally be under the remit of the Careers Teacher, the wise Head of Department would see a number of enhanced possibilities for specific pupils.

- The development and use of resources from the local community, be they museums, books, people, sites, etc. can bring about significant benefits in motivation and attitude. It is always important, however, to ensure that pupil enquiries are focused and purposeful.

- Involving people from the community in school, such as the involvement of the transport manager of a local firm in a geography project about the location of an out of town shopping centre.

- Class visits which are built into the curriculum by detailed advance planning, with effective follow through.

- Using mentors from the community to support pupil/class work.

- Experts in residence, widely used in Drama and English

- Virtual contacts through databases and comms links such as the Internet and conferencing by audio, Email and video.

- Informing the local library about topics involved in current or preferably future project work.

- In all these situations, there is a lot to be gained from an orchestrated approach across the department so that those pupils with the greatest need can be targeted effectively.

- Agencies that can be approached for assistance can include:
  - The local Educational Business Partnership or EBP
  - Local Industry
  - Individuals with specific skills
  - People within the school community with unusual skills, such as the technician with a hobby of animal husbandry
  - Local TEC /LECs
  - Community Service Volunteers

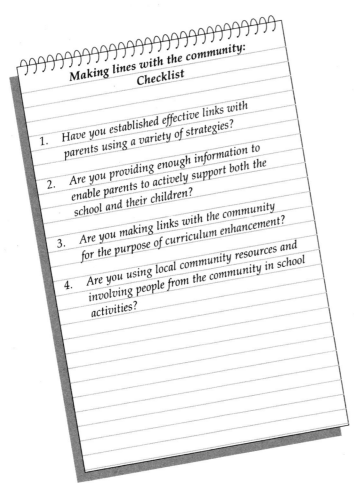

Making lines with the community: Checklist

1. Have you established effective links with parents using a variety of strategies?

2. Are you providing enough information to enable parents to actively support both the school and their children?

3. Are you making links with the community for the purpose of curriculum enhancement?

4. Are you using local community resources and involving people from the community in school activities?

Monitoring and Evaluation

In Section Seven you will learn that:

☞ *Monitoring and evaluation are important and can be achieved by*

- *classroom observation*
- *pupil work analysis*
- *analysis of examinations*
- *pupil interviews*

Why is it that monitoring and evaluation always appear at the end of the agenda? Somehow they are often included as afterthoughts, yet if we are looking seriously at management issues, classroom practice or curriculum or development planning, it is crucial to be able to assess and make judgements about performance in order to be able to inform future practice. To be able to do this effectively requires the processes of monitoring and evaluation to be set up at the onset of the work in hand, so that they can be incorporated appropriately and with minimum distortion to the learning. In short, before we start on a journey we need to know what the destination looks like so we will know when we have arrived.

The process of monitoring is something that at a basic level we all do intuitively, especially when we finish a particularly disastrous or good lesson. Of course the real trick is to spend some time reflecting on why it happened the way it did, and which of the variables in the situation could we control in a future situation. Evaluation on the other hand takes a longer view, and will often take into account a wider range of data. The techniques involved in both monitoring and evaluation cover the same range of possible instruments and so will be considered together for the rest of this chapter.

Monitoring and evaluation are increasingly recognised as important because:

- ✎ schools exist in an accountable society where they are increasingly subject to external scrutiny.
- ✎ they help departmental teams to judge whether they are meeting the aims they have set themselves.
- ✎ they provide departments with real insight into poor and effective areas of achievement.
- ✎ they make sure that planned changes are based on real rather than assumed needs.
- ✎ they help ensure scarce funds are wisely spent.
- ✎ they help focus the professional development provision of departments.
- ✎ they help departments to ensure greater consistency in their provision.
- ✎ they help ensure success receives recognition.
- ✎ they help teachers cope with external monitoring and evaluation such as school inspection.

A Head of Department can involve colleagues in the monitoring/evaluation process by the use of one or more instruments.

- classroom observation and review.
- pupil work analysis.
- analysis of assessment results.
- pupil interviews.

Whichever instrument is chosen, the manner of its introduction needs to be managed in such a way that all those involved feel comfortable with its application. As Professor Brighouse suggests in his introduction to this series, lessons which are planned by one teacher but taught by another, and observed by the former can be just one way of reducing the stress levels involved.

With all the instruments outlined above due consideration must be given to the costs involved (time, cover, materials, etc.) together with the extent, if any, of the disturbance to the learning process.

Classroom observation and review

Classroom observation needs a clear and agreed set of purposes, restricted foci and publicly understood feedback processes. It is time consuming and requires careful preparation and expertise but it is most effective way of evaluating:

- relationships between teacher and pupils and among pupils.
- the balance of praise and criticism.
- the quality of learning.
- the effectiveness of provision for the less and more able.
- the pace of work.
- questioning strategies.
- the clarity of explanations.
- the level of challenge provided.
- the extent to which problem solving is deployed.
- whether time is well used.

When the focus of the observation has been decided, it is generally necessary to draw up a detailed chart for recording the data. It is often best to be as specific as possible, and to limit the variety of data and the number of pupils involved, as in the example on page 59.

Alternatively useful classroom observation techniques are set out in, '*School Based Classroom Activities*' by **Oldroyd D., Smith K. and Lee J., Longmans /Schools Council.**

Work Analysis

Work analysis is best conducted collaboratively, by all the teachers responsible for a given year group sitting down together with exercise books or folders and completing an agreed proforma. It can provide information on:

- Whether work schemes are being followed
  - Is the balance of time allocated appropriate?
  - Is the National Curriculum covered?

Sample Classroom Observation Schedule

School	Class	Date	Time
Class/Group	Teacher	Researchers	

		1	2	3	4
Grouping	Individuals				
	Whole Class				
	Small Groups				
	Pairs				

Teacher Talk

		1	2	3	4
Inform	Task Input Session (providing information)				
	Non-Task Input				

		1	2	3	4
Instruct	Instructions - task				
	Instructions - non-task				

		1	2	3	4
Questioning	Closed factual related to curriculum				
	Open ended - curriculum				
	Non-task				
Purpose of questioning - task	Shape learning				
	Formal Assessment				
	Monitoring progress				
	Establish prior knowledge				

		1	2	3	4
Feedback	Score/mark				
	Behaviour (positive/negative)				
	Comments - standards of work (positive/negative)				

Non-talk categories

		1	2	3	4
Teacher role	Helping with task				
	Input new information				
	Shaping/development learning				
	Formal assessment				
	Informal assessment/monitoring of learning				
	Verbal feedback				
	Recording pupil's progress and achievement				
	Gathering information from records of progress and achievement				
	Routine housekeeping/discipline				

		1	2	3	4
Teacher position	At board				
	Mobile				
	A a central base				
	At pupil base				
	At own desk/base				

Leicester University, Phase 3, 1996

✎ Whether departmental policy / practice on assessment is being adhered to
- Are students receiving constructive advice?
- Are targets being set?
- Are poor quality outcomes being challenged?

✎ Whether work undertaken is sufficiently varied
- Are students carrying out sufficient high-order tasks?
- Is a blend of resources being used?

✎ Whether work is sufficiently detailed
- A sample of exercise books / folders from another school can be a useful point of comparison.

✎ Whether students are being required to take some responsibility for their own learning
- Are students planning and undertaking independent research work?
- Are students being required to take decisions about order presentation, format, content?

✎ Whether there is an appropriate balance of knowledge and skills development

✎ Whether differentiation strategies are effective
- Are students' outcomes sufficiently different?
- Are some students undertaking work that is different in kind?

✎ Whether the more able are being extended
- Do they always do all the basic activities expected of the less able?
- Does extension work provide something different or merely more of the same?

Analysis of assessment results
This can be perceived as threatening, particularly if badly handled or launched onto a team which is unconvinced of its value and wary of its purpose. However, it can be very effective if:

✎ an open and accepting culture has been established within the department.
✎ it understood to the starting point in discussing and reviewing a topic not the finished outcome.
✎ a like for like basis is used for comparisons (e.g. how did these students do in the other subjects they took? How well did our students do compared to students in very similar schools?)
✎ there is not an over reliance on end results such as GCSE and A Level grades obtained, (some internal results such as end of Yr 10 examination results or estimated grade data can be acted upon whilst the students are still in the school).

Pupils Interviews

Pupil interviews are an under-used technique which can provide useful and often surprising data. They can generate nonsense, 'We would work much harder if we were paid'.' Or real insight, 'It's annoying to have the work explained all over again when you already understand it and the teacher is really only talking to two people.'

Useful questions include:

- Which work have you been particularly proud of? Why?
- Which work have you been dissatisfied with? Why?
- What helps you work well?
- What frustrates you when you are working?
- What activities do you do most?
- Which activities do you do least?

It is important to make sure that students know the discussion is not an opportunity to denigrate individuals, whether teachers or other students. It is equally important to ensure colleagues are confident that such denigration will not be tolerated. Repeated interviewing of students will be undermined if the students perceive there are no responses to what they are saying.

The quality of inforrmation gained by pupil interviews is well illustrated in *'Flexible Learning: The Evidence Examined'* by **Mike Hughes, NEP, 1994.**

Alternatively, a Head of Department could use a questionnaire with a sample of pupils. The following questionnare has been used to identify the variety of learning activities that pupils experience.

	Rarely	Sometimes	Often	Frequently
How often do you work on your own?				
Copy from the board?				
Work with computers?				
Work in pairs				
Go on trips?				
See a television programme?				
Listen to the teacher?				
Ask questions?				
Work in small groups?				
Copy from a book?				
Work with members of the opposite sex?				
Use the library?				

In one school pupils were given this questionnaire prior to the introduction of a teaching and learning styles exercise. They were then asked to complete it again at the end of the trial and results were compared.

It is important to ensure that the monitoring process has credibility. As already indicated, correct professional conduct is essential. Furthermore, action must be seen to be taken on what is learnt from the process. That not only reinforces what you have done - it gives a recognised value to future monitoring procedures.

Monitoring and Evaluation: Checklist

Monitoring / Evaluation works best when:

1. It concentrates on big issues.

2. The method chosen matches the area to be reviewed.

3. It routinely involves the whole team rather than concentrating on poor performance.

4. The values, purposes and processes are understood and shared by the whole team.

5. It is undertaken in small, manageable amounts.

6. There is sensitivity about 'comfort zones' and territories.

7. The middle manager is prepared and committed to act on the results.

8. Positive outcomes are followed up on just as effectively as negative ones.

9. Results are openly discussed and seen as starting points not end outcomes.

10. Self review and evaluation are important elements.

11. An outside perspective is added (e.g. an LEA inspector/adviser).

12. Previous monitoring has been 'validated' by the results being acted upon.

Section Eight

Teaching and Learning

In Section Eight you will learn that:

☞ **Effective Heads of Department need to focus on teaching and learning by:**

- **creating high teacher expectations**
- **developing planned variety**
- **providing challenge in lessons**
- **establishing a problem solving climate**

An effective Head of Department sets out to focus the collective efforts of the team upon central, significant activities. A huge range of activities take place within any school, but it is obvious that two activities are vital above all others - teaching and learning. Effective departments have realised this and understood that they are two things they need to be good at. They therefore concentrate their efforts upon them. In order to bring this about, a Head of Department should seek to:

✎ establish ways in which good ideas about teaching and learning are regularly and routinely exchanged and communicated within the team (e.g. items such as work sheets and lesson plans are pinned on the department notice boards).

✎ organise department meetings so that they always devote significant time to planning, reviewing and evaluating the teaching and learning taking place.

✎ ensure that time is not wasted on the discussion of dead or fixed issues which have already been determined elsewhere (i.e. provide the wisdom to help the team realise that some issues are simply not worth arguing further over).

Teachers exhibit a range of different 'persona' in the classroom. Some function as 'enablers', some as 'ring masters' and some as 'entertainers'. Many change roles from class to class or within the course of a lesson with the same class. A wise Head of Department recognises the presence of these different persona and does not seek to impose one fixed departmental style. To do so can lead to unproductive interference in areas which teachers will see as part of their individual autonomy and limiting of their personal creativity. What an effective middle manager should be attempting is to create departmental emphases or themes which are not dependent upon the personality of teachers but which do have a critical impact on the quality of teaching and therefore learning.

Successful departments tend to be characterised by a Head of Department providing the drive and energy for high quality and leadership in the following key areas:

- ✎ Creating high teacher expectations
- ✎ Developing planned variety
- ✎ Providing challenge in lessons
- ✎ Establishing a problem solving climate.

Creating High Expectations

Teachers demonstrate high expectations by:

- ✎ the degree of difficulty of the work they set.
- ✎ clearly communicating success criteria to children which describe what good work should look like.
- ✎ challenging low quality work and responses either orally or through marking.
- ✎ insistence upon personal best standards for individual children.
- ✎ creating and tolerating thinking time, especially during question and answer sessions therefore encouraging depth of response.
- ✎ requiring justifications for pupils' answers.
- ✎ creating a can-do culture including 'talking up' successes of students.
- ✎ providing a strong role model, for example through the quality of resource materials given to students.
- ✎ insistence upon orderly and constructive behaviour.
- ✎ rigorously praising and valuing work or behaviour of genuine high quality.

Teachers' expectations can be viewed as fixed, static points, (perhaps a product of their previous teaching or learning experiences) or as factors which can be impacted upon by effective discussions and INSET.

An effective Head of Department will go to great lengths to praise high expectations and achievements in addition to encouraging teachers to see any lower expectations as variable which are subject to movement.

This can usually be best achieved by providing:

Challenge to any negative stereotypes which are used in discussions. →	This is a constant 'battle' but one in which even teachers' casual. apparently humorous, comments should not be ignored.
A high but realistic indication of what results could be achieved by the department. →	This needs to be informed by the succes gained in other departments of the same school or in departments in similar schools (visits to other schools can be the best way to do this).
Discussions about what constitutes good quality work can be very helpful in this respect. →	This ensures that success criteria are effectively communicated to students.

● Feedback and advice to individual teachers about:

their questioning strategies →	so that they are not reliant on short answer, memory-recall questions but instead provide a range of questions which require in-depth thinking and response.
their balance of praise and criticism →	so that teachers can realise the overall messages they convey to students. Are they positive but demanding?
their willingness and effectiveness in challenging low quality work →	this is a critical area of teacher intervention
the extent to which they create high, individualised expectations geared to students' abilities →	in order to help them judge the effectiveness of their classroom differentiation
the extent to which they create condtructive atmosphere for learning →	in order to judge whether poor behaviour is inhibiting learning
the quality of resources they use with students. →	do they set difficult tasks and signal high expectations?

Obviously feedback and advice of this type is only possible if systematic monitoring takes place. Providing detailed and direct observation of the teacher is perhaps the most difficult role of all but one which many good middle managers have taken on successfully.

Developing Planned Variety

Teachers adopt very different stances on variety in their classroom.
"Children need routines. You can't vary things too much or they get lost."
"Well... variety happens naturally doesn't it."
"Variety is the single most important factor in my teaching."

What is clear is that variety is a key in boosting pupil motivation. It is also clear that, if we don't counteract it by clever teaching, children acquire inflexibility. Put another way one of the teacher's most important roles is teaching pupils to be flexible and cope with change by providing them with a variety of learning situations. An important role of a Head of Department is therefore to help teachers develop greater awareness of the variety they currently provide and then to help them plan for and deliver as wide a range as is feasible.

Variety can be provided through:

   ✎   changes in seating arrangements.
   ✎   adjusting pupil grouping.

- ✎ using a range of different kinds of resources.
- ✎ regular inclusion of stimulating 'set piecing' activities such as fieldwork, drama and role play.
- ✎ routinely use a range of different learning activities, especially those which require high order as well as low order learning.

The proforma **'Towards Planned Variety'** (see page 67) provides one means to record, monitor and review variety. It is also frequently helpful for teams to brainstorm the full list of teaching and learning strategies available to them. That list can act as a powerful aide memoire and can then be 'ordered' from the most demanding 'high order' activities of a given child or perhaps for two or three different children in the manner indicated. The tracking sheet 'High and Low Order Activities' (see page 68) is a sample of this kind of device.

It is feasible for an individual to use this as an aid to planning or later as a self reviewing exercise. Alternatively a team might jointly review the effectiveness of a unit of work by using exercise books or folders as an aide memoire and check the experiences of students over perhaps the last month's work. It is easy for a Head of Department to develop a false view of the variable being provided by the department

It is important to review variety from the point of view of what an individual child experiences and not simply by looking at the range provided across the department.

Providing challenge in Lessons

The word challenge is similar to the word counselling in the wide range of different meanings it holds for teachers. Among all the different understanding what is clear and generally agreed upon is that challenge is an important element which can greatly influence the quality of what happens in a classroom. Challenge is vital to the development of self-esteem. The key is to balance challenge with success.

HIGH CHALLENGE + LOW SUCCESS	= FAILURE
LOW CHALLENGE + HIGH SUCCESS	= PATRONISED
HIGH CHALLENGE + HIGH SUCCESS	= SELF-ESTEEM

It is the role of a head of department to help the team develop a common awareness of the many ingredients which can help to provide intellectual challenge to pupils. The checklist 'Providing Challenge in Lesson' provides material which could be used in the departmental discussions and as a basis for INSET. The review questions can be used in a range of ways, by teachers as appraisal foci, as means of self review, or by middle managers to assist with their lesson observations of colleagues.

It is clear that teachers have further range of sophisticated means of making work more demanding. They do so in the way they subtly use different tones of voice, by their facial expressions, even by the way they tolerate silent thinking time. The role of a Head of Department is to help teachers to become more aware of their many, often intuitive strategies in order that they use them progressively more effectively. Book 2 in this series, *'Effective Learning Activities'* sets out a model for the design of challenging work in lessons.

TOWARDS PLANNED VARIETY

Group being tracked		Ability		Time Period	

Sources

Model making	☐☐☐☐☐
Game	☐☐☐☐☐
Role/simulation	☐☐☐☐☐
Debate	☐☐☐☐☐
Discussion	☐☐☐☐☐
Drama/play	☐☐☐☐☐
Individual research	☐☐☐☐☐
Paired group research	☐☐☐☐☐
Drawing/illustration	☐☐☐☐☐
Planning	☐☐☐☐☐
Decision making	☐☐☐☐☐
Essay	☐☐☐☐☐
Diary	☐☐☐☐☐
Extended reading	☐☐☐☐☐
Brainstorm	☐☐☐☐☐
Diagrammatic work	☐☐☐☐☐
Graph work	☐☐☐☐☐
Statistical work	☐☐☐☐☐
IT use	☐☐☐☐☐
Visits/field work	☐☐☐☐☐
Practical work	☐☐☐☐☐
Pen/paper questioning	☐☐☐☐☐
Copying	☐☐☐☐☐

Sources

Info sheet	☐☐☐☐☐☐☐☐☐
Info booklet	☐☐☐☐☐☐☐☐☐
Photographs	☐☐☐☐☐☐☐☐☐
Text book	☐☐☐☐☐☐☐☐☐
Map/diagram	☐☐☐☐☐☐☐☐☐
Range of books	☐☐☐☐☐☐☐☐☐
Newspapers	☐☐☐☐☐☐☐☐☐
Library	☐☐☐☐☐☐☐☐☐
Fieldwork	☐☐☐☐☐☐☐☐☐
Demonstration	☐☐☐☐☐☐☐☐☐
Audio	☐☐☐☐☐☐☐☐☐
Video	☐☐☐☐☐☐☐☐☐
Computer	☐☐☐☐☐☐☐☐☐
CD Rom	☐☐☐☐☐☐☐☐☐
Other adults	☐☐☐☐☐☐☐☐☐
Community	☐☐☐☐☐☐☐☐☐

Format of work

Individual folder	☐☐☐☐☐☐☐☐☐
Exercise book	☐☐☐☐☐☐☐☐☐
Paper - larger format	☐☐☐☐☐☐☐☐☐
Poster	☐☐☐☐☐☐☐☐☐
Display	☐☐☐☐☐☐☐☐☐
IT output	☐☐☐☐☐☐☐☐☐
Audio tape	☐☐☐☐☐☐☐☐☐
Video	☐☐☐☐☐☐☐☐☐
Drafting employed	☐☐☐☐☐☐☐☐☐

Room Layout

Individual desks	☐☐☐☐☐
Desks in pairs	☐☐☐☐☐
Desks in small groups	☐☐☐☐☐
Desks in large groups	☐☐☐☐☐
'Board meeting'	☐☐☐☐☐

Audience

Teacher only	☐☐☐☐☐☐☐☐☐
Other pupils this group	☐☐☐☐☐☐☐☐☐
Pupils' other groups	☐☐☐☐☐☐☐☐☐
Other adults	☐☐☐☐☐☐☐☐☐
Home	☐☐☐☐☐☐☐☐☐

Pupil 'Grouping'

Individual	☐☐☐☐☐☐☐☐☐
Pupil chosen pair	☐☐☐☐☐☐☐☐☐
Teacher chosen pair	☐☐☐☐☐☐☐☐☐
Pupil chosen group	☐☐☐☐☐☐☐☐☐
Whole class	☐☐☐☐☐☐☐☐☐
Mixed ability	☐☐☐☐☐☐☐☐☐
'Setted' groups	☐☐☐☐☐☐☐☐☐
Mixed gender groups	☐☐☐☐☐☐☐☐☐

☐ - should be used to record dates used

High and Low Order Activities

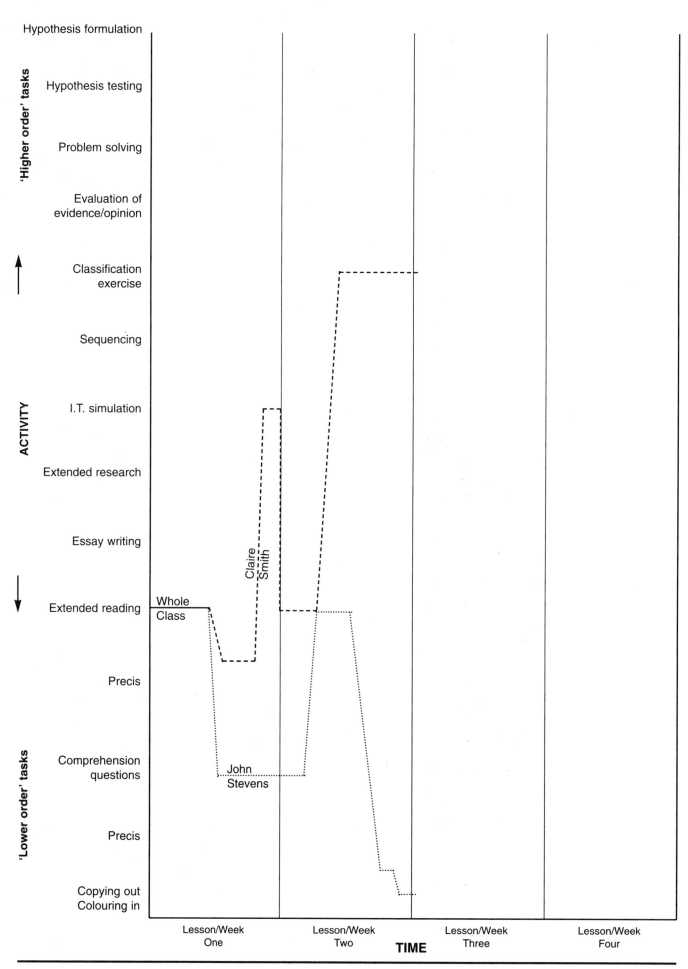

A review checklist for middle managers and teachers.

Questioning strategies

- Are questions of varied type and length?
- Are open ended questions such 'what might happen if...?" or "how might you....?" used
- Are students required to justify the answers they give?
- Are all students draw into the Q and A process
- Is thinking time tolerated and encouraged by the teacher?

Interventions and interactions with students

- Are interventions/interactions concerned overly with classroom management rather than improving understanding?
- Are interactions always triggered by the students? (e.g. by the lack of understanding or poor behaviour)
- Does the teacher intervene to encourage depth and detail?
- Does the teacher effectively challenge low quality outcomes from students?

Target Setting and the use of criteria

- Are clear quality (not time) target set and pursued?
- Are the characteristics of a high quality piece of work made clear to students?
- Do feedback and marking routinely set targets for future achievements?

Pace

- Are time target (including short steps targets) provided for students?
- Are time targets pursued without compromising depth of student response?
- Are lessons structured to provide motivational carrots in the later sections and therefore encourage students to work with some pace?

Grouping

- Do social groupings always prevail?
- Does the teacher create and vary groups which will at times allow students of similar abilities to work together (e.g. are the most able sometimes paired/grouped to take on more difficult tasks)?

High order and low order tasks

- Is a variety of learning activities planned into the lesson?
- Does the lesson contain an appropriate blend of high order tasks (such as evaluation of hypothesis formulation) in addition to normal low order activities (e.g. comprehension questions)?
- Does the lesson structure ensure that less able students do access some higher order activities?
- Does the lesson structure ensure this?

Differentiation

✎ Is the prior knowledge of students used to inform the different work they undertake?

✎ Do the students understand and respond to the different expectations that the teacher has of them?

✎ Are strategies in place to ensure the most able are extended by moving on to different kinds of work (i.e. they do not just do more of the same)?

✎ Are the less able presented with tasks in which they can gain success?

✎ Does the teacher effectively challenge any evidence of an 'achievement-shy' culture?

Homework

✎ Does homework simply involve completion of class activity (and thereby risk not extending those who have worked more quickly in the lesson)?

✎ Is homework matched to the range of abilities of students present in the class?

Problem solving

✎ Do lessons include the use of a range of resources including difficult 'first hand' materials?

✎ Has the teacher created a climate in which students strive to solve problems for themselves rather than depend upon the teacher?

✎ Does the lesson ensure worthwhile and detailed engagement with the topic being studied or simply coverage of the content?

Expectations

✎ Is the lesson specifically planned to ensure that students know/ understand/can do something better/differently by the end of the lesson?

✎ Does the teacher clearly signal high expectations to student?

✎ Are students expected to perform to their own individual best level or only to the level of those around them?

Creating a Problem Solving Climate

However astute a teacher is at prediction, examination papers will always confront students with problems they have never faced before.

However impressively retentive a student is in his/her learning, life beyond school will throw up a barrage of situations which require problem solving skills rather than simply an excellent memory of acquired facts. Thus a key role of a Head of Department is to ensure that lessons include problem solving activities and that problem solving activities and a problem solving climate are created across their department.

There are a range of things which teachers do which can inadvertently limit the extent of problem solving in their classroom. These include:

- allowing students to sit in their own chosen social group rather than providing the challenge of them having to work with different people in different contexts.
- providing one resource from which students can obtain all the answers they need.
- answering students' questions with full and complete answers rather then channelling students' thoughts back into answering the question for themselves.
- always providing a framework for students to work to (eg graphs with axes already labelled) so that they do not have to create them for themselves.
- providing 'coverage' of syllabus topics rather then in depth engagement with the main issues.

An effective Head of Department will work with their team to help ensure that:

- wherever practical a range of resources are provided including 'first hand' materials e.g. satellite photos (collaborating planning and sharing are the keys here).
- students are required to ask questions as well as answer them. (An approach involving 'What would you ask.......... to find out more about...?' can be used in very many contexts). See Book 4 in this series, *'Lessons are for Learning'* for a detailed discussion of ways to promote questioning students.
- when teacher elaborate upon the requirements of a task they only do so to students who need it (a Head of Departments's role is to ensure that teachers do not take away the challenge in a task by over explanation or by explaining something to a whole class when only some students require the assistance).
- research tasks are part of the diet of work done by all students (these can be brief focused tasks like requiring students to look up a spelling in a dictionary or much lengthier extended investigations).
- work is not simply equated with writing in the minds of students or teachers (whilst writing may help retention, thinking is the key problem solving activity).
- 'problems' are seen as productive areas for investigation rather than negative factors.
- teachers build problems into their planning of work rather than solve all the problems in advance before students even meet them.
- students are required to take meaningful decisions about their work (not just about presentation but about its planning, organisation and perhaps assessment).

Finally, the pace and amount of recent change has added further dimensions to the Head of Department role. Firstly, it is important to prioritise - to judge which changes are far-reaching and likely to be longer lasting, as opposed to those which are both peripheral and ephemeral.

The Head of Department has to calculate the impact of these changes for the department. How are they to be managed? How are they to be introduced and implemented? Are there any considerations to be given to resourcing, assessment procedures, teaching and learning styles etc.

The Head of Department then has to ensure the integration of new developments within the existing ethos of the department. His/her team should have the opportunity to consider the implementation of the change within the framework of the department's professional philosophy and judgement. Which of our procedures is congruent to the changes? Which require modification? In what way should we modify?

Whatever the outcome, the proactive Head of Department will have communicated and managed the change in a way that respects and values the expertise of their staff and their key role in change implementation. After all it is their expertise which creates interesting, effective and happy learning environments.

In relation to teaching and learning, the vital questions a Head of Department might ask are:

Teaching and Learning: Checklist

Am I:

1. Creating a department 'culture' in which teaching and learning are consistently seen as the environment activities?

2. Ensuring departmental time and energy are focused on those activities?

3. Monitoring classroom provision to provide the team with information about their
   - expectations of students
   - the variety of activity they provide
   - the challenge they give to students
   - classroom climate?

4. Providing teachers with wisdom and 'the tools' to review their own classroom especially in relation to the four main areas above?

5. Ensuring that discussion, debate and training focuses on the areas of need uncovered by monitoring and self review?

6. Encouraging teachers to discuss and share their own professional judgements in establishing creative, interesting and stimulating teaching and therefore effective learning?